HIGH QUEST

Name	
Address	
Phone	**Email**

www.highquest.info

HIGHQUEST II - His Image

v.3.31

ACKNOWLEDGEMENTS

The Navigators is an international Christian organization whose calling is to advance the Gospel of Jesus Christ into the nations through spiritual generations of laborers living and discipling among the lost. (www.navigators.org/us)

HighQuest is a ministry of The Navigators Church Discipleship Ministry (CDM) which is focused on helping churches become more intentional in disciple making. CDM staff nationwide are available to help church leadership develop the critical components that will enable them to accomplish Christ's Great Commission. For additional help contact: The Navigators, Church Discipleship Ministries, PO Box 6000, Colorado Springs, CO 80934 - or call (719) 594 2446

HIGHQUEST DESIGN TEAM: Ron Bennett, Larry Glabe, Chuck Strittmatter, Bob Walz

HighQuest: Men on a Mission logo designed by Bob Walz
The cross represents the gospel of God's kingdom and the sword the Word of God. Each is essential for the quest.

Cover photo is licensed from artzooks.com

Unless otherwise noted all Scripture taken from the HOLY BIBLE: NEW INTERNATIONAL VERSION®, NIV®. Copyright © 1973, 1978, 1984 by International Bible Society. Used by permission of Zondervan Bible Publishers.

His Image is one unit in the *HighQuest: Men on a Mission* series. For further information regarding this material and other discipling resources go to: www.highquest.info

HighQuest [Men on a Mission]: His Image
ISBN: 978-0-9823829-1-2
ISBN: 0-9823829-1-x

TABLE OF CONTENTS

HIGHQUEST II: HIS IMAGE

The Quest

A "quest" could be defined as a "journey with adventure". Following Christ is the ultimate quest; it is more than just a trip. In a trip, like a vacation, we leave from point A, travel to point B, and return back to point A. Along the way, we take pictures, buy souvenirs, and share experiences. A trip creates memories but not changed lives.

A quest involves leaving point A and heading to point B without making plans to return. A quest results in life change. We never recover from a quest. Following Christ is a journey that involves both leaving what is behind and pressing on to what is ahead.

Can Real Men Walk With a Real God in a Real World?

Our journey of faith in Christ does more than make memories; it involves adventure. It is a journey with drama. There is nothing boring about following Christ in His kingdom. Adventure, drama, beauty, excitement, and hardship are part of the high quest of following Christ for a lifetime. You are invited to take your next step in this exciting journey.

"In light of all this, here's what I want you to do. ... I want you to get out there and walk—better yet, run!—on the road God called you to travel. I don't want any of you sitting around on your hands. I don't want anyone strolling off, down some path that goes nowhere. And mark that you do this with humility and discipline—not in fits and starts, but steadily, pouring yourselves out for each other in acts of love" (Ephesians 4:1-2 MSG).

The Mission of HighQuest

> **The HighQuest mission is to equip men to:**
> • Know Christ deeply
> • Reflect Christ authentically
> • Share Christ intentionally

Equipping Men

Equipping means "to prepare by training or instruction." It is different than teaching. While teaching is important, equipping is essential. While teaching provides information, equipping provides skills.

In order for men to follow Christ for a lifetime, they need to be trained to face the challenges that lie ahead in the journey. Learning and practicing core skill sets (or spiritual disciplines) are essential, if a man is to walk effectively and authentically with Christ over the course of his life.

Becoming equipped consists of acquiring the proper skills and tools in order to face an ever-changing landscape with confidence. A lack of proper training and equipment results in fear and frustration. Being properly equipped means having the right concepts, principles, tools, and skills to walk with a real God in a real world.

• Know Christ Deeply

Most men find their identity in their accomplishments, titles or positions. Our lives are spent trying to prove our competence while living in constant fear that we will someday be found out and exposed. But what if our lives were based not on **what** we did but on **who** we know? Jesus said in John 17:3, "Now this is eternal life: that they may know you, the only true God, and Jesus Christ, whom you have sent."

The Bible's perspective is that knowing Christ is both our greatest privilege and our greatest challenge. God has put within the heart of every man the desire to know Him. The desire may be masked by the callousness of indifference, the cloud of sin, or the compulsion of busyness, but it is there.

Paul fanned the spark by letting go of the fickle facade of status and achievement, to focus on knowing Christ.

"What is more, I consider everything a loss compared to the surpassing greatness of knowing Christ Jesus my Lord, for whose sake I have lost all things. I consider them rubbish, that I may gain Christ…I want to know Christ and the power of his resurrection and the fellowship of sharing in his sufferings, becoming like him in his death" (Philippians 3:8, 10)**.**

Knowing Christ is the heart of our journey of faith. Everything flows from this one relationship which consists of more than believing facts about Christ. It is the personal, progressive process of walking with Christ through all of life's situations. Knowing Him demands honest and consistent communication with him through the shared experiences of normal everyday living.

Knowing Christ is the incredible privilege of a personal friendship with the living God. In John 15:5, Jesus told his disciples, "I no longer call you servants …instead I have called you friends." Friendship with God is not a relationship of equals. It is, however, the awesome opportunity for children to relate to their heavenly Father. As we learn, believe, and obey the will of God, he reveals more of his heart to us through his Spirit.

• Reflect Christ Authentically

Historically church leaders have agreed that the primary purpose of our lives is to glorify God. But glorifying God is not in its essence, the common practice of singing worship songs or thinking mystical thoughts. We glorify God as we reflect his revealed nature through our everyday, ordinary lives.

"And we, who with unveiled faces all reflect the Lord's glory, are being transformed into his likeness with ever-increasing glory, which comes from the Lord, who is the Spirit" (2 Corinthians 3:18).

We reflect Christ as we are transformed in character, values, beliefs, and behavior. This inside-out transformation shapes our new identity in Christ and makes us authentic. We are becoming who we really are.

As the moon reflects the light (glory) of the sun, so we are to reflect the light (glory) of God. We, like the moon, are dependent on an external source for light. As we grow to know him and our lives change to conform to his image, we become lights to those around us. "You are the light of the world," Jesus said. God wants to display his nature to the world by transforming the lives of men of faith.

Reflecting Christ requires a partnership in which God's Spirit works in us as we cooperate with him. Our response to God's Word is one of faith and obedience. The result is we are transformed to be more and more like Christ. We value what he values. We make our ways his ways. We make his truth our beliefs.

• Share Christ Intentionally

God's plan is to reach people through people. We are like links in a chain. Each spiritual generation is a link to the next. Jesus said to His disciples during his final hours on earth,

"You did not choose me, but I chose you and appointed you to go and bear fruit—fruit that will last" (John 5:16).

He made a similar statement in Matthew 4:19 when he said, "Follow Me and I will make you fishers of men" (NASB).

Following Christ naturally leads to fishing for men. "Fishing for men" (spiritually investing in others) is our part in adding new links to the spiritual chain.

God's strategy for reaching people with the good news of his love is through people. When Jesus gathered his disciples together after the resurrection, he gave them this mission:

These few, ordinary men turned their world upside down. They launched a world-changing movement without the aid of technology, political clout or social status. They did it one person at a time.

> *As you are going, make disciples!* **Matthew 28:19**

The Components of HighQuest

Each HighQuest unit has two components: life skills and life issues. The life skills are developed around life issues.

• Life Skills

Each HighQuest unit helps develop core skills or disciplines that a man needs to walk with God for a lifetime. Each skill is an historical spiritual discipline that has been used by believers of all ages and cultures for the purpose of developing spiritual maturity.

In any area of life, skilled habits can make us more effective. Those who have developed the skill of a smooth golf swing have greater freedom on the golf course. Men who have developed the skill sets of an effective conditioning program have greater freedom to engage in various physical activities. A doctor who has developed surgery skills has greater freedom in the operating room. The skills themselves are not the goal but the means to something greater.

Spiritual habits are avenues of God's grace that allow us to tap into His power. They result in increased freedom to experience Christ. New skills, however, do require time and practice to become habits. At first they even seem mechanical and awkward, but with persistence, the new skills will become a natural part of your lifestyle. Then you will be free to focus on your relationship with Christ rather than the discipline.

Paul knew that spiritual disciplines were important. He told Timothy, "Do not waste time arguing over godless ideas and old wives' tales. Spend your time and energy in training yourself for

spiritual fitness. Physical exercise has some value, but spiritual exercise is much more important, for it promises a reward in both this life and the next" (I Timothy 4:7-10 NLT).
He also reminded the young believers in Corinth of his own commitment to discipline and why it was important to him.

"Do you not know that those who run in a race all run, but only one receives the prize? Run in such a way that you may win. And everyone who competes in the games exercises self-control in all things. They then do it to receive a perishable wreath, but we an imperishable. Therefore I run in such a way, as not without aim; I box in such a way, as not beating the air; but I buffet my body and make it my slave, lest possibly, after I have preached to others, I myself should be disqualified" (I Corinthians 9:24-27 NASB).

Spiritual training -- developing the habit of spiritual disciplines -- is absolutely necessary for our journey with Christ.
The following life skills are developed in the HighQuest series:

HighQuest I: Meeting with God
HighQuest II: Gripping the Scripture
HighQuest III: Investing your life

• Life Issues

Each HighQuest unit will look at a key life issue. These life issues are foundational concepts on which you will need to build your life. HighQuest will only give you an introduction to these important topics, but with the skills you learn, you can continue to explore and develop these and other life issues on your own or with a few other men in a HighQuest Forum.

It is important to realize that understanding and wisdom come as we depend on the Holy Spirit and dig into the Scripture as if looking for buried treasure. The Bible is not written as a text book or an encyclopedia. Topics are not neatly arranged and conveniently located. The Bible speaks to every issue we will face in life but in the context of the stories of real people; people

HIGHQUEST II: HIS IMAGE

who have traveled their own high quest.

The Scripture is both an autobiography of God as he reveals himself through history and a life application manual. God reveals principles and truths that teach us how to live life effectively. His principles are timeless. His truth is always true. The story line of the Bible is set in a particular culture at a particular time in history, but the teaching is ageless. Jesus said that, "Heaven and earth will pass away. But my words will never pass away" (Matthew 24:35).

Learning to go to the Bible for answers to life's questions is a mark of a disciple of Christ. Knowing that God has spoken and will speak to you is a mark of faith. As you search the Scripture, depend on the Holy Spirit as your guide and instructor. He will not just speak to your mind but to your heart as well.

His Image

HIGHQUEST II
SET UP SESSIONS

The focus of this Set Up Session is to get acquainted as a forum and understand what *HighQuest II: His Image* is all about.

1. Begin by getting acquainted with the men in your forum. Each man should share his contact information on page 11 so the others can record it.

2. If this is a new group or there are new people in the group,
a. Each man should share his Personal Profile (pages 12-15) so others can learn and record it.
b. Each man should fill out and share their Personal Time Line on page 21.

3. Review the material on a HighQuest Forum on pages 16-20. Emphasize that each week during your Forum, each person will be sharing from their AWG journal and their Check the Map.

4. Review the fundamentals of an AWG (page 22) along with how to fill out the Check the Map (page 23). A full explanation of an AWG is found in the Appendix (pages 128-132).

5. Read the introduction to *His Image* (pages 24-25).

Name

Address

Phone   Email

Name

Address

Phone   Email

Name

Address

Phone   Email

Name

Address

Phone   Email

Name

Address

Phone   Email

PERSONAL PROFILE

NAME

FAMILY

BIRTH DATE   **ANNIVERSARY**

PLACES LIVED

SKILLS/HOBBIES

JOB HISTORY

FIRST CAR

NICKNAME

12

NAME

FAMILY

BIRTH DATE   **ANNIVERSARY**

PLACES LIVED

SKILLS/HOBBIES

JOB HISTORY

FIRST CAR

NICKNAME

PERSONAL PROFILE

NAME

FAMILY

BIRTH DATE   **ANNIVERSARY**

PLACES LIVED

SKILLS/HOBBIES

JOB HISTORY

FIRST CAR

NICKNAME

NAME

FAMILY

_____
_____
_____
_____

BIRTH DATE   ANNIVERSARY

PLACES LIVED

_____

SKILLS/HOBBIES

_____
_____
_____

JOB HISTORY

_____
_____
_____
_____
_____
_____

FIRST CAR

NICKNAME

_____

Forum Essentials

The HighQuest forum is an environment in which 3-4 men meet for perspective, encouragement, and accountability.

> ### Most men tend to live lives that are:
> - *isolated rather than connected*
> - *compartmentalized rather than integrated*
> - *disengaged rather than engaged*

In order to deal with these issues, the HighQuest Forum creates a consistent place where men can be listened to, taken seriously, and understood.

There are four essentials of a HighQuest Forum: Connection, Exploration, Application, and Intercession. Each one is a vital part of the Forum experience.

• Connection

The operative question for the beginning of each HQ Forum is *"Because we care, what do we need to know?"*

Most men are asking the question, "Who knows and who cares?" The HighQuest Forum creates a safe environment in which men can relate with one another on a deeper level than news, weather, and sports. It is safe because each man is given the opportunity to honestly discuss real and relevant issues in his life and still be accepted and respected by the other men. It is also safe because nothing is shared outside the HighQuest Forum without permission.

There are additional reasons why the HighQuest Forum is ideal for 3-4 men.
1. It allows time for everyone to participate in a 60-90 minute format.
2. It gives greater flexibility for meeting locations: home, office, or restaurant.

• **Exploration**

The operative question is *"Because God's Word is true, what are you discovering?"*

Every man needs to learn how to feed himself from the Word of God. Passivity is devastating for men on a quest with God. Most men learn best when they are involved in the process of discovery. Passively listening to the truth of God's Word as it is taught by others, is like a man in a canoe with no paddle. His ability to navigate the river is extremely limited. But when you give him the skills to discover truth for himself, you equip him to travel the waterways of truth for the rest of his life.

Most men lack confidence to personally go to the Bible and gain insight for their lives. In HighQuest men develop the skills needed to explore and gain understanding from God's Word. In addition, the HighQuest Forum gives an opportunity to share personal insights as well as learn from others.

• **Application**

The operative question is *"Because God's Word is relevant, what is He telling you to do?"*

In order to follow Christ on this journey, men need more than insight. They need application. Application takes the truths of the Bible and integrates them into the fabric of life. We mature as we apply God's truth to our personal, family, and professional life.

Spiritual truth must not be isolated to a spiritual compartment of life while most of our thoughts and energy go into the business of everyday living. God's plan is to integrate his truth into our everyday, ordinary lives. There is no isolated spiritual compartment -- just spiritual men living real life in a real world.

The HighQuest Forum is an environment where men are loved and accepted yet challenged to change. Men need a "band of brothers" who will stand up for them and to them: men who will challenge them to do what is right and celebrate when they do it.

• Intercession

> The operative question is *"Because God cares, how can we support you in prayer?"*

The HighQuest Forum includes personal prayer for and with each other. Holding up each other in prayer is a critical force for encouragement and power. Sharing needs and victories together in the context of prayer, builds a connection and puts the focus on God's work in our lives.

Praying together is often the most difficult part of the High-Quest Forum. It is important not only for men to pray for each other during the week but also during the HighQuest Forum. Not everyone will be comfortable praying in a group. The leader will need to be flexible and responsive to the backgrounds of the members. However, as the group develops a greater level of honesty and transparency, prayer usually becomes a less formal and more relaxed part of the HighQuest Forum experience.

Using a conversational style of prayer allows member to participate at their own comfort level. The leader will need to guard this prayer time as it can easily become absorbed by the other parts of the HighQuest Forum.

Forum Format

A forum is like a rope that is woven together from separate strands. Each component is a strand that gives strength to the whole. It is important that you use the whole rope during each forum. A forum will not be effective if strands are missing. The forum facilitator will need to govern when to move to the next component.

The best way to keep moving is simply to ask the next operative question. Avoid letting one part dominate. This doesn't mean you have to spend the same amount of time on each question. For example, some weeks critical issues raised in the group may cause you to spend more time on intercession. Allow the Holy Spirit freedom to lead the group but maintain cohesion and direction.

A typical HighQuest Forum meets for 60 minutes. The hour can be divided into the following strands:
(If you have 90 minutes, simply expand each strand by 50%)

- **Connection: 15 minutes**
- **Exploration: 25 minutes**
- **Application: 10 minutes**
- **Intercession: 10 minutes**

Forum Ground Rules

It is important to establish some simple yet critical guidelines for your forum. These basic ground rules will create the security and trust that men need if they are to become honest, vulnerable, and transparent.

- I will commit to the group; make attendance to the weekly Forum a priority.
- I will be willing to be transparent and encourage other

members of the group to do likewise.
- I will complete the assignment for the week and be ready to share with the group.
- I will hold (in confidence) the personal matters shared in the group.

Signed: _____

Forum Discussion Notes

As you meet each week in your HighQuest Forum, you will be covering: Connection, Exploration, Application and Intercession.

At the end of each weekly journaling session, there is a page for taking notes during your forum. This page allows you to record thoughts and ideas that others share during the discussion.

FORUM DISCUSSION

CONNECTION	
"Because we care, what do we need to know?"	

EXPLORATION	APPLICATION
"Because God's Word is true, what are you discovering?"	*"Because God's Word is relevant, what is He telling you to do?"*

INTERCESSION	
"Because God cares, how can we support you in prayer?"	

SPIRITUAL JOURNEY TIMELINE

+

−

You were born

You are here

In HighQuest I: Knowing Christ Deeply, you learned how to have an AWG using the outline of Read, Record, Reflect, and Respond. You will continue to use that format in this unit of HighQuest.

Developing the life skill of meeting with God on a regular (preferably daily) basis takes effort and time. We do not learn new habits quickly. But once we learn them, they allow us to focus on the result more than the process. We hope your AWG will become a lifelong habit on your quest with Christ. As you gain greater skill in the use of the AWG, you will gain greater freedom to modify it and make it fit your personality and life style without losing the essential ingredients.

In this unit of HighQuest, you will not be taught how to have an AWG, but you will be given the opportunity to re-inforce what you have already learned and become more consistent. If you have not developed the life skill of an AWG, we suggest you refer to one of the units in HighQuest I before continuing with this unit.

Remember, the given passages are not to limit you but to start you. You may read more or less than suggested. The AWG is designed to allow you to listen to and dialogue with God. As you read and God speaks through his Word, stop and listen. Your AWG is to help you connect with Christ on a regular and personal basis; to sit at his feet and listen to his words.

By now the mechanics of an AWG should be fading into the background allowing you to focus on your time in Christ's presence. The key to meeting God in His Word is to ask three core questions: What does it say? What does it mean? How can I apply it? The AWG format in HighQuest was designed to help you think that way.

HighQuest: His Image is laid out in a six-day sequence with the sixth day to "check the map." The Check the Map page is a way to review what God has been teaching you and make application.

One way to review is to take key ideas from the daily AWGs and list them on the Check the Map page. Once you have all ideas written down, summarize by stating the central theme or big idea. You may also review by focusing on one specific day that stood out to you. Write down summary thoughts from that day looking for one big idea that brings focus to the week.

Personal application

Responding to what God is revealing to you through His Word is the most critical part of the journey. Writing out an application is a way to move from the conceptual to the practical; from information to transformation. Make your application a way to act on what you have heard God say. Make it specific, short term and measurable. Remember, the most profound application is often a very simple one.

In this unit of HighQuest we are focusing on reflecting Christ's nature through specific traits. Consider the following steps as you reflect on how to build these traits into your life:

1. **Express** the trait in your own words. What does this trait look like in action?

2. **Reflect** on how Jesus demonstrated it. Think about how Jesus expressed this trait during his life.

3. **Assess** your personal demonstration of this trait. Examine this trait in your own life as you look at the various roles you have (husband, dad, friend, worker, etc). Confess where you see yourself falling short and where you want to develop.

4. **Claim** his power and promises to make this trait evident in your life. Ask God to show you where and how to demonstrate this trait.

5. **Apply** this trait in specific situations that you face right now. Consider your natural roles or networks: family, marketplace, neighborhood, etc. What can you do this week to make this trait more evident?

Introduction: His Image

The goal of spiritual transformation is to reflect Christ. As the gospel spread from Jerusalem into the Gentile world, a new church was established at Antioch. Not only did a large number believe but their lives were changed. Luke records in Acts 11:26 (NASB),

"And it came about that for an entire year they met with the church, and taught considerable numbers; and the disciples were first called Christians in Antioch."

The term Christian means "Christ-one" and clarifies the term "disciple." It was created to describe those believers who reflected the ideas, values, character, and behavior of Jesus. They were shaped by him and reflected him. The term has lost its original meaning today but the principle remains. Those who follow Christ will become like him.

Jesus, using the Jewish concept of disciple, said in Luke 6:40, "A pupil is not above his teacher; but everyone, after he has been fully trained, will be like his teacher."

Our tendency is to conform to a culture, even a Christian culture. But anything short of Christ-likeness is a poor substitute and fails to realize who we are in Christ. Peter refers to this new image by calling it our divine nature.

"Seeing that His divine power has granted to us everything pertaining to life and godliness, through the true knowledge of Him who called us by His own glory and excellence. For by these He has granted to us His precious and magnificent promises, in order that by them you might become partakers of the divine nature, having escaped the corruption that is in the world by lust" (2 Peter 1:3-4 NASB).

He further delineates this divine nature by identifying core qualities:

"Now for this very reason also, applying all diligence, in your faith supply moral excellence, and in your moral excellence, knowledge; and in your knowledge, self-control, and in your self-control, perseverance, and in your perseverance, godliness; and in your godliness, brotherly kindness, and in your brotherly kindness, love. For if these qualities are yours and are increasing, they render you neither useless nor unfruitful in the true knowledge of our Lord Jesus Christ" (2 Pet 1:5-8 NASB).

Paul uses the expressions "put off" and "put on" to refer to this process of inner change.

"That, in reference to your former manner of life, you lay aside the old self, which is being corrupted in accordance with the lusts of deceit, and that you be renewed in the spirit of your mind, and put on the new self, which in the likeness of God has been created in righteousness and holiness of the truth."
Ephesians 4:22-24

In this unit of HighQuest, we will be looking at some qualities of our new nature. The transformation into the likeness of Christ is a lifelong journey. It takes our attention and focus to continually put on our new nature. In this unit, we want to get a clearer picture of the image of Christ as we seek to reflect him authentically.

As you read each passage, keep in mind that the topic for the week is not the only subject in that passage. However, each passage will speak to the weekly topic either directly or indirectly, and provide "cross references" for your meditation. Reflecting on these passages will expand your understanding of the verse you are memorizing.

The focus of this Set Up Session is to become familiar with the Life Skills of Scripture Memory and Planned Meditation that will be part of your AWGs.

1. Read and discuss Gripping the Scripture on pages 27-28.

2. Read and discuss the skills for successful Scripture memory on page 29.

3. Read and discuss the parts to Planned Meditation on pages 31-37.

4. Do the practice Planned Meditation on pages 38-41.

5. Assignment: Begin your AWG using Session 1 on page 46.

Gripping the Scripture

Mountain climbing requires the skill of attaching secure points in the snow or rock along the route to serve as anchors. Pitons are wedged into the cracks of rocks and ice screws are used in snow. Carabineers are then attached to these anchors giving the climber a secure point to attach his rope. Solid points of attachment are critical for a safe and successful climb.

Setting anchor points in Scripture is also necessary for a successful journey with Christ. In *HighQuest track* II, we will be teaching you how to get a grip on the Scripture so you can firmly attach yourself to God's truth as an anchor along your journey. Getting a grip on Scripture requires the combination of memory and meditation.

In an age of Smart Phones, computers and a myriad of bible translations, Scripture memory has become a lost art. In the days before the printing press, few people had access to written material. Only the educated elite would own or access books. Memorizing was practiced as much for necessity as for its inherent value.

In track II of the *HighQuest* series, we have selected the verses for you. Each verse is key for the given topic. Later, you will need to identify and select your own verses based on the issues you face. As you spend time in the Word God will highlight verses to reflect on. Use what you learn in *HighQuest* to get a grip on the Word and anchor yourself to the truth.

As you experience the value of **memorizing** Scripture and combine it with the habit of planned **meditation**, you will have a skill set that equips you for the life long journey.

• Memorizing

You may be thinking, "So why memorize Scripture today when I can read it on my Smart Phone in a matter of seconds?" The answer lies not so much in the head but in the heart. It is not so much a question of how much of the Scripture do we have but rather how much does the Scripture have of us?

Scripture memory secures the Word of God deep into our

hearts where the Holy Spirit can use it to pull us up to new heights. Memorizing Scripture lends stability to our lives on treacherous terrain and slippery slopes. Possessing the skill of using it can be the difference between a serious fall and a successful climb.

You may have memorized Scripture in the past for a variety of external reasons that have not held up in your adult world. Memorizing Scripture is often treated as a kid's thing that is not relevant for adults. But when you discover how to grip God's word through the combination of memorization and meditation, you will find one of the most powerful skills for life transformation.

The Bible gives us some practical reasons why we should memorize Scripture or "hide it in our hearts" as was the Old Testament expression. As you learn the skill of Scripture memory and begin to enjoy its benefits, you will discover that each of these benefits will touch your life at some time. Here are a few to consider.

Memorization Benefits
1. Victory over sin: Psalm 119:11
   "I have hidden your word in my heart, that I might not sin against you."
2. Think correctly: Philippians 4:8
   "And now, dear brothers and sisters, let me say one more thing as I close this letter. Fix your thoughts on what is true and honorable and right. Think about things that are pure and lovely and admirable. Think about things that are excellent and worthy of praise."
3. Worship: Psalm 119:164
   "I will praise you seven times a day because all your laws are just."
4. Guidance: Psalms 119:24
   "Your decrees please me; they give me wise advice."
5. Prayer: John 15:7
   "But if you stay joined to me and my words remain in you,

you may ask any request you like, and it will be granted!"

6. Counseling: Isaiah 50:4
"The Sovereign Lord has given me his words of wisdom, so that I know what to say to all these weary ones. Morning by morning he wakens me and opens my understanding to his will."

Memorization Principles

Look over the following suggestions for effective Scripture memory. Regardless of your natural ability to memorize, you may be able to get a verse into your short term memory in a matter of a few minutes. However, it takes regular practice and review to retain it.

1. Select a good translation to memorize from (NIV, NKJ, NASB, etc).
2. Before you start to memorize a verse, read it aloud several times.
3. Write out the verse on a small card so you can carry it with you. (In HighQuest II, the verses are printed in the back of the book.)
4. Learn the topic, reference, and first phrase as a unit. Memorize the verse word for word.
5. Repeat #4 and add a phrase at a time until you have the entire verse. Always quote the reference before and after you quote the verse.
6. Repeat the verse out loud several times a day.
7. Keep the verse with you and review it 4-5 times as you go through the day.
8. Quote the verse to someone who will listen.
9. Review each verse at least once a day for 7 weeks.

LIFE SKILL: SCRIPTURE MEMORY

The most critical element in Scripture memory is review, review, review! The most important time to review a verse repeatedly is right after you can quote the whole verse from memory (topic, reference, verse, reference) without making a mistake. Review the verse at least once a day, preferably several times each day. The more you review, the greater the retention.

Thorough learning is an important concept. A verse should not be considered memorized when you can quote it accurately. Only when you have reviewed it every day for 7 weeks will it be ingrained in your memory.

In *HighQuest: His Image,* you will memorize 5 verses. As you memorize a new verse, you will need to review the old ones as well. The goal is that at the end of this unit, you will be able to quote all 5 verses word perfect at one time. For a list of verses you will be memorizing, go to the chart on pages 42 and 43.

The memory verses are also in the back of this unit so you can cut them out and carry them with you.

Meditation
(From The Navigators *Primer on Meditation*)

"'Meditation is simply thought prolonged and directed to a single object. Our mystic chambers where thoughts abide are the secret workshop of an unseen Sculptor chiseling living forms for a deathless future. Personality and influences are modeled here. Hence, the Biblical injunction 'Keep your heart with all diligence, for out of it are the issues of life.'

A. T. Pierson

Meditation is chewing. It is like the graphic picture of a cow and her process of mastication. It involves bringing up previously digested food for renewed grinding and its preparation for assimilation. Meditation is pondering and viewing various thoughts by mulling them over in the mind and heart. It is the processing of mental food. We might call it "thought digestion." "Chewing" upon a thought deliberately and thoroughly, thus providing a vital link between theory and action. What metabolism is to the physical body of the cow, meditation is to your mental and spiritual life.

Meditation is analyzing. It is the art of taking a good, long look at a given object as the craftsman does his dazzling jewel...polishing the diamond to reflect all its light and beauty. Meditation on a portion of the Holy Bible is like gazing at a prism of many facets, turning the stones from angle to angle in the bright sunlight. Steady and constant reflection reveals unlimited beauties from the Scriptures which will never otherwise be seen. "Open my eyes to see the wonderful truths in your law" (Psalms 119:18 NLT).

Meditation is action. Someone has described it: "Making words into thoughts and thoughts into actions." It is mentally planning ahead with definite action in mind for accomplishing a job.

"Muse" was the name given to an ancient Greek god who spent much time in solitude and thinking. The statue of "The Thinker" is the artistic concept of deep concentration and absorption. Add an "a" to the beginning of "muse" and you have:

LIFE SKILL: Planned Meditation

"amuse—sports, games, television and a score of other tools used by the enemy to keep God's men from concentrating on man's God.

Beware of getting alone with your own thoughts. Get alone with God's thoughts. There is danger in rummaging through waste and barren desert thoughts that can be labeled—day dreaming or worse. Don't meditate upon yourself but dwell upon Him—seek God in your inner thought life. There is always danger in meditating upon our problems. Develop the habit of reflecting upon the Word of God and therein find the answers to your problems."[1]

"You satisfy me more than the richest of foods. I will praise you with songs of joy. I lie awake thinking of you, meditating on you through the night" (Psalm 63:5-6 NLT).

Planned Meditation

In HighQuest II, we will be using Planned Meditation (PM). This form of meditation includes four specific steps that will guide the meditation process in an inductive manner. Thinking inductively involves taking things apart before putting them back together into a conclusion. Deductive thinking starts with the conclusion and works back to the parts. The inductive form of meditation starts by asking "What does it say?" followed by "What does it mean", and concluding with "How can I apply it?"

When meditation is added to the skill of Scripture memory, God's Word becomes more than knowledge. It allows the Spirit to access the deepest part of our soul and results in transformed lives. The writer of Hebrews said,

"For the word of God is full of living power. It is sharper than the sharpest knife, cutting deep into our innermost thoughts and desires. It exposes us for what we really are. Nothing in all creation can hide from him. Everything is naked and exposed before his eyes. This is the God to whom we must explain all that we have done" (Hebrews 4:12-13 NLT).

1 A Primer on Meditation, The Navigators

An important principle of meditating on Scripture is to understand the context of the verse in question. The context is the setting in which a statement (or verse) is made. Often we misinterpret a verse because we fail to understand the context. The context is found by looking at what is said before and after the verse on which we are meditating. This may involve reading a paragraph or even a chapter. In this unit of HighQuest II, we have designed your AWG passages to incorporate the context of the verse you are memorizing.

Another principle of meditation is to "interpret Scripture by Scripture." This means looking at other parts of the Bible to add insight and understanding. This part of meditation is called "cross referencing". The more time you spend in the Bible, the easier it will be to find cross references. Some Bibles have a cross reference list in the page margin or in an index at the back. Cross references may be on a word, concept or idea.

This HighQuest unit has passages for your AWG that are cross references for the verse you are memorizing. Some of these passages are examples; others amplify the words or ideas in the verse you are memorizing.

Although the passages selected for your AWG are tied to a theme, don't worry if you don't always make the connection. Remember that your AWG is an opportunity to listen to God. Listen first and connect what you hear to the selected theme second.

Planned Meditation Steps (see sample page 36-37).
1. Writing the verse
Begin your planned meditation by writing out the verse (from memory if you can). You can use this step to check your memory and it will serve as a visible reference later.

2. Defining key words
Identify each significant word in the verse. Using a dictionary, write down all relevant definitions for each word. A dictionary can expand our normal understanding of a word and lead to

new insight. Try reading the verse using a word definition or synonym.

If you have access to a Biblical dictionary like the Vines New Testament Word Study," you can also find some additional insight into word meanings.

3. Saying it again

Write out the verse in your own words. Use what you have discovered from the definitions above to say it differently yet not losing any of the meaning. This could be called your paraphrase.

4. Breaking it down

Now you should reflect on the verse for greater understanding. You have been looking at what it says, now look for what it means. One way to meditate to gain understanding is to ask questions. Questions can help us see new patterns and relationships.

- **See:** Make observations as to what is being said. Look for the main ideas or concepts. Look for the connections between thoughts and ideas. Be an explorer or detective. The more you look, the more you will see.

- **Search:** Look for answers to the questions: Who? What? Where? Why? How? Some of these questions will be answered in the verse itself, others may be implied. Look for additional insight from some of the passages you used in your AWG to answer your questions. Be bold in asking questions even if you don't come up with answers.

- **So what:** The "so what?" question helps you turn knowledge into practice. It keeps you from remaining theoretical. You want to think in terms of how Scripture can relate to real life. It involves asking an if/then question such as, "If what I have observed is true, what difference would/should it make? How could it relate to my family, neighborhood, marketplace or personal life? "

Try expressing it this way, "If _____ (state the truth), then _____ (state the implication).

There are always a number of implications for any discovered truth. Some may be relevant to where you are and others may be relevant later.

5. Finding the bottom line

Write a statement that summarizes what you think is the main principle or idea of the verse. This is an objective statement which answers the question "What is this verse saying?" or "Why did God include this verse in Scripture?"

6. Putting it into Action

You will apply this verse to your life using the "Check the Map" page in your AWG section. This step involves identifying the key truth God is impressing on your heart and then looking for a way to put that truth into action.

PLANNED MEDITATION

Write it out (Copy it from your Bible)

"I am the vine; you are the branches. If a man remains in me and I in him, he will bear much fruit; apart from me you can do nothing."

Define key words (Use a dictionary)

VINE: (grapevine): A plant with a woody stem that bears grapes

BRANCH: Any woody extension growing from a trunk: any part or extension of a main body

REMAIN: To be left when the rest has been taken way; to stay in the same place; to continue, go on being; endure, persist.

FRUIT: Product: a plant product: the result, consequence or product of any action.

NOTHING: nonexistence; insignificance or non important; vain useless; of little or no value, trivial

Say it again (Put it in your own words)

Jesus says, "I am the trunk and you are the branches. If you stay connected to Me, you will be fruitful. Without My life giving resources, you will dry up and be useless."

Write it out *(Copy it from your Bible)*

"*I am the vine; you re the branches. If a man remains in me and I in him, he will bear much fruit; apart from me you can do nothing.*"

Break it down *(See, Search & So What?)*

Jesus is clarifying the relationship I have with Him. I am dependent on the vine for nourishment. The vine is the source, support and anchor for the branches. Fruit is not automatic. The "if" word makes it conditional The condition is my choice to remain in the vine. There is freedom to disconnect but the results will be fruitlessness.

Remaining in or continuing in means to persevere... not just temporary or periodically. What is the "fruit"? It could be the character of Christ i.e. fruit of the Holy Spirit or it could be good works or deeds. Jesus gives the results of remaining and not remaining. Failing to remain in Him results in activity but stuff of little value or importance. It's not that we can't do something but that it amounts to nothing of any real value.

Find the bottom line *(The main principle)*

God's plan is to produce fruit through me. He is a ready source of divine poser but I must choose to remain vitally connected to him. I can live without this union with Him but it will result in activity without significance. motion without meaning.

37

PLANNED MEDITATION

As you begin HighQuest II, it will be beneficial to practice together this new life skill of Planned Meditation (PM). To do this, follow the practice plan below and fill out the Planned Meditation forms on pages 40 and 41. The verse you will use is 2 Peter 1:4. This verse is from one of the passages you will look at in your AWG this week.

One of the study skills you will use is defining key words in the verse. Because you probably do not have a dictionary with you, the definitions for key words in 2 Peter 1:4 are listed on the next page. Normally a good English dictionary will be adequate for gaining insight into key words. You may also like to use a Bible dictionary like *Vines Complete Expository Dictionary of New Testament Words* or *Vincent Word Studies*. In *His Nature* there are two parts to the planned meditation. You will do one part each week. In this practice exercise, you will do both at once.

Planned Meditation Practice (page 40-41)

1. **"Write it out."** Copy 2 Peter 1:4 from your Bible.

2. **"Define key words."** Identify the key words in the verse and write down (highlight in this exercise) definitions. Refer to the definitions listed for you on the next page. Share your insights with the group.

3. **"Say it again."** Write out 2 Peter 1:4 in your own words using insights from your definition of key words. This becomes your "paraphrase" of the verse. Share your paraphrase with your group.

4. **"Break it down."** Review the explanation of how to break it down on page 34. Write down a few of your observations. As a group, share insights and observations from the verse.

5. **"Find the bottom line."** Write down a summary of what this verse means to you. Have a few men in the group share their summary with the others.

Precious
1. Of high cost or worth; valuable   2. Highly esteemed; cherished 3. Dear; beloved

Promise
1. A declaration assuring that one will or will not do something; a vow 2. Something promised

Participate
1. To take part in something 2. To share in something

Divine
1. Having the nature of or being a deity 2. Heavenly; perfect

Nature
1. The essential characteristics and qualities of a person or thing 2. The fundamental character of a person

Escape
1. To break loose from confinement; get free; escape from jail
2. To avoid a serious or unwanted outcome

Corruption
1. Lack of integrity or honesty use of a position of trust for dishonest gain 2. In a state of progressive putrefaction
3. Moral perversion; impairment of virtue and moral principles; moral degeneracy

World
1. The system of life (beliefs, values, ethics and practices) marked by self-reliance and independence from God

Write it out *(Copy it from your Bible)*

Define key words *(Use a dictionary. Page 33)*

Say it again *(Put it in your own words. Page 34)*

Write it out (Copy it from your Bible)

Break it down (See, Search & So What? Page 34)

Find the bottom line (The main principle. Page 35)

Session	Topic/AWG Passages	Memory
1	**From Old to New (A)**	**Romans 12:2**
Day 1	Romans 12:1-8	
Day 2	2 Corinthians 3:12-18	
Day 3	2 Peter 1:3-11	
Day 4	Romans 8:1-11	
Day 5	Planned Meditation Part 1 (Romans 12:2)	
Day 6	Check the Map	
2	**From Old to New (B)**	**Review Romans 12:2**
Day 1	Matthew 5:1-20	
Day 2	Galatians 5:16-26	
Day 3	Ezekiel 36:24-32	
Day 4	2 Corinthians 10:1-6	
Day 5	Planned Meditation Part 2 (Romans 12:2)	
Day 6	Check the Map	
3	**From Anger to Patience (A)**	**James 1:19**
Day 1	James 1:19-27	
Day 2	Ecclesiastes 7:1-14	
Day 3	Ephesians 4:25-32	
Day 4	Psalm 37:1-11	
Day 5	Planned Meditation Part 1 (James 1:19)	
Day 6	Check the Map	
4	**From Anger to Patience (B)**	**Review James 1:19**
Day 1	1 Peter 2:18-25	
Day 2	1 Samuel 25	
Day 3	Proverb verses	
Day 4	Matthew 5:21-26, 38-48	
Day 5	Planned Meditation Part 2 (James 1:19)	
Day 6	Check the Map	
5	**From Anxiety to Peace (A)**	**Philippians 4:6**
Day 1	Philippians 4:1-9	
Day 2	Luke 12:22-34	
Day 3	Isaiah 40:21-31	
Day 4	Luke 10:38-42	
Day 5	Planned Meditation Part 1 (Philippians 4:6)	
Day 6	Check the Map	
6	**From Anxiety to Peace (B)**	**Review Philippians 4:6**
Day 1	John 14:23-31	
Day 2	Isaiah 26:1-12	
Day 3	Mark 4:1-20	
Day 4	Psalm 27	
Day 5	Planned Meditation Part 2 (Philippians 4:6)	
Day 6	Check the Map	

Session	Topic/AWG Passages	Memory
7	From Pride to Humility (A)	Philippians 2:3
Day 1	Philippians 2:1-11	
Day 2	James 3:13-18	
Day 3	1 Peter 5:1-11	
Day 4	Luke 18:9-14	
Day 5	Planned Meditation Part 1 (Philippians 2:3)	
Day 6	Check the Map	
8	From Pride to Humility (B)	Review Philippians 2:3
Day 1	James 4:1-12	
Day 2	Philippians 2:19-30	
Day 3	John 13:1-17	
Day 4	Ephesians 4:1-6	
Day 5	Planned Meditation Part 2 (Philippians 2:3)	
Day 6	Check the Map	
9	From Sexual Immorality to Purity	1 Thessalonians 4:3
Day 1	1Thessalonians 4:1-8	
Day 2	Proverbs 6:20-35	
Day 3	Genesis 39:1-23	
Day 4	1 Corinthians 6:9-20	
Day 5	Planned Meditation Part 1 (1 Thess. 4:3)	
Day 6	Check the Map	
10	From Sexual Immorality to Puritey(B)	Review 1 Thess. 4:3
Day 1	2 Timothy 2:4-26	
Day 2	1 Peter 1:13-21	
Day 3	Psalm 51	
Day 4	1 John 3:1-10	
Day 5	Planned Meditation Part 2 (1 Thess. 4:3)	
Day 6	Check the Map	

His Image

HIGHQUEST II
APPOINTMENT WITH GOD JOURNAL

"Under Construction", would be an appropriate statement to wear on the front of a believer's sweatshirt. We need the reminder that God is in the process of remodeling our lives to fit his design. The back of the same shirt, might read "Built to last." Paul said in 1 Corinthians 3 that once the foundation of Christ is laid, the builder must use materials that will stand the test of time and inspection.

When Jesus promised eternal life to those who would put their faith in him (John 3:16), he was referring to more than life after death. The cross of Christ is the foundation for a whole new life experience that begins at the moment of personal faith and lasts for eternity. Our foundation in Christ results in God's instantaneous gift to us which includes forgiveness, inheritance, adoption, and the indwelling of the Holy Spirit.

This Christ foundation also begins God's work in us. This work involves a process of real change from the inside out. We start to become what we really are. We are made holy, and we are now becoming holy. We are sons of God (I John 3:1-3) and we are being changed to look like it. What God does for us happens in an instant, but what God does in us takes a lifetime.

Paul reminds us that we have a part to play in the "re-construction" process. In Philippians 2:12 he says, "So then, my beloved, just as you have always obeyed, not as in my presence only, but now much more in my absence, work out your salvation with fear and trembling" (NASB). He is not saying that we are working for our salvation but working it out i.e. letting it find expression through our individual lives.

Romans 12:2 is a key verse that captures the concept of life change using the term "transformation." Your AWG readings this week will give you additional passages to expand your understanding of what it means to be "Under Construction."

READ

RECORD

REFLECT

RESPOND

RECORD

REFLECT

RESPOND

READ

RECORD

REFLECT

RESPOND

FROM OLD TO NEW
2 PETER 1:3-11

Day 3

_____

_____
_____
_____
_____
_____
_____
_____
_____
_____
_____
_____

_____
_____
_____
_____
_____
_____
_____
_____
_____
_____
_____

_____
_____
_____
_____
_____
_____
_____
_____

READ

RECORD

REFLECT

RESPOND

Write it out *(Copy it from your Bible)*

Define key words *(Use a dictionary. Page 33)*

Say it again *(Put it in your own words. Page 34)*

LIFE APPLICATION

1. Express
2. Reflect
3. Assess
4. Claim
5. Apply
(see page 23)

FORUM DISCUSSION

"Because we care, what do we need to know?"

EXPLORATION

"Because God's Word is true, what are you discovering?"

APPLICATION

"Because God's Word is relevant, what is He telling you to do?"

INTERCESSION

"Because God cares, how can we support you in prayer?"

The Greek word for "transformation" is the word from which we get our word "morph." It is used to describe spiritual, inside-out change. (Other parallel words are "maturity", "growth", "formation", and "discipleship.") Transformation is not a Biblical equivalent of "Extreme Makeover." It is not primarily outward redecorating but is predominantly an inward change process. Transformation touches our hearts. We can adapt or modify our behavior and not be transformed. Transformation changes our values, attitudes, beliefs, and character, as well as our behavior.

The direction of spiritual transformation is towards the image of Christ. We are to become more like him. Jesus said that a pupil, when fully trained, will be like his teacher. Even the antagonistic religious authorities recognized this life change in the early apostles.

"The members of the council were amazed when they saw the boldness of Peter and John, for they could see that they were ordinary men who had had no special training. They also recognized them as men who had been with Jesus" (Acts 4:13).

Spiritual transformation requires an interrelated cooperation between God and us. Much of the instruction of the New Testament is directed towards our part of that process. Although the entire transformational journey from beginning to end is based on God's grace, he has given us a path to walk that unleashes his power in our lives.

The Holy Spirit uses ingredients like his Word, prayer, and obedience, along with the pressures of every day living, to produce this lasting change. Change that is authentic is rarely instantaneous; most often it is frustratingly slow. Usually if we want change at all, we want it now. But God seems content to use an old fashioned crock-pot rather than a modern microwave.

RECORD READ

REFLECT

RESPOND

READ

RECORD

REFLECT

RESPOND

READ

RECORD

REFLECT

RESPOND

Write it out *(Copy it from your Bible)*

Break it down *(See, Search & So What? Page 34)*

Find the bottom line *(The main principle. Page 35)*

LIFE APPLICATION

1. Express
2. Reflect
3. Assess
4. Claim
5. Apply
(see page 23)

CONNECTION

"Because we care, what do we need to know?"

EXPLORATION

"Because God's Word is true, what are you discovering?"

APPLICATION

"Because God's Word is relevant, what is He telling you to do?"

INTERCESSION

"Because God cares, how can we support you in prayer?"

Road rage! Sports rage! Domestic rage! Workplace rage! Evidence of anger is everywhere. It's hard to tell if we are actually becoming more angry or simply feeling a greater freedom to express it. Violent acts of anger are simply the tip of the iceberg. Most men are able to suppress the rage that makes the evening news. But just below the surface, the anger is still there.

Many naively think they can cover it up but, it tends to leak out in any number of subtle and destructive ways. Some men control their anger in the public arena only to unload it on family and friends. Wives and children become easy targets of stuffed anger. Those we love most can become the unsuspecting targets of days--even years--of fermenting anger.

Anger gets expressed in many creative and destructive ways. Some are physical and others verbal. Criticism and withdrawal are passive forms of anger that may seem innocent but inflict great pain.

Anger is much like the oil light on the dashboard of the car. When the light goes on, it alerts us to a problem deep within and out of sight--a problem that, if ignored, will cause major damage. Covering up the light or simply getting used to it being on will only lead to greater maintenance bills in the future. Dealing with the real issue is the best way to respond to the anger indicator.

Perceived rights and thwarted goals are common sources of anger. When these rights and goals are consistently challenged, anger can easily turn into rage or revenge.

The Biblical solution to anger is neither to ignore it nor to vent it. God teaches us to deal with anger at its source. As you read and reflect on the passages for this week, listen to what light God brings to your heart as you learn to move from anger to patience.

READ

RECORD

REFLECT

RESPOND

63

READ

RECORD

REFLECT

RESPOND

READ

RECORD

REFLECT

RESPOND

Write it out *(Copy it from your Bible)*

Define key words *(Use a dictionary. Page 33)*

Say it again *(Put it in your own words. Page 34)*

CHECK THE MAP

LIFE APPLICATION

1. Express
2. Reflect
3. Assess
4. Claim
5. Apply
(see page 23)

CONNECTION

"Because we care, what do we need to know?"

EXPLORATION

"Because God's Word is true, what are you discovering?"

APPLICATION

"Because God's Word is relevant, what is He telling you to do?"

INTERCESSION

"Because God cares, how can we support you in prayer?"

Managing anger is a worthy and necessary step but not the ultimate goal. The ability to control feelings of anger and direct them away from destructive behavior is a mark of maturity. A tantrum thrown by a two year old is not unusual or alarming. However, a tantrum thrown by a 22 (or 42) year old, should be a matter of concern.

As children of God, Scripture teaches that we are not to be victims of our emotions. Paul reminds Timothy that he did not have the spirit of fear but of love and self control. God's Spirit has set us free from sin and its slavery to the flesh. Moving from anger to patience involves choosing to act in ways that are loving, forgiving, and healing. But if we only learn to manage our anger and not to change it, we are missing real spiritual transformation.

Spiritual transformation replaces anger with patience. Patience, someone once joked, is that quality you appreciate in the driver behind you but dislike in the one ahead. The word for patience in the Bible literally means "abide under." Parallel words are "longsuffering," "endurance," and "fortitude." Patience involves the ability to wait, persevere and bear up under adverse conditions.

Jesus modeled patience as he continually dealt with a hostile world. Unjustly accused, maligned, and misrepresented, Jesus responded with loving patience. Even when the disciples failed to understanding and believe, Jesus didn't respond in anger. Patience was not just an act but part of his very nature. He didn't appear patient just because he had self control. He was patient.

It is not enough to just control our anger. Transformation means actually becoming patient. When God changes our hearts, we won't have to count to 10 to avoid becoming angry…not even 1 or 2. Patience simply becomes who we are in the image of Christ.

RECORD **READ**

REFLECT

RESPOND

READ

RECORD

REFLECT

RESPOND

READ RECORD

REFLECT

R SPOND

PROVERBS 10:12; 14:17,29; 15:1,18;
16:32; 19:11; 22:24-25; 29:11

Day 3

READ

RECORD

REFLECT

RESPOND

Write it out *(Copy it from your Bible)*

Break it down *(See, Search & So What? Page 34)*

Find the bottom line *(The main principle. Page 35)*

LIFE APPLICATION

1. Express
2. Reflect
3. Assess
4. Claim
5. Apply
(see page 23)

CONNECTION

"Because we care, what do we need to know?"

EXPLORATION

"Because God's Word is true, what are you discovering?"

APPLICATION

"Because God's Word is relevant, what is He telling you to do?"

INTERCESSION

"Because God cares, how can we support you in prayer?"

Anxiety reigns in our world, where bankruptcies are mounting, companies are downsizing, and families are disintegrating. Pressures seem unrelenting. Just as one issue is resolved, several more appear. The Biblical command, "Don't be anxious about anything," seems impossible.

Anxiety saps emotional, mental, and physical strength through stress, fear, and loss of sleep. If left unchecked, anxiety can result in emotional and physical breakdown, along with countless missed opportunities.

Because anxiety in a man's heart weighs him down, men seek release through a variety of activities and involvements that promise big but deliver little. There may be temporary relief but no lasting peace.

Anxiety is quite revealing. It almost always reveals a spirit of self reliance—an "it all depends on me!" way of thinking. Being in control is what drives us. We can actually become quite content with independence until we discover a glitch in our armor. Our health fails, the pink slip arrives, or our children leave home in anger. Even if these things don't happen, they could! Even if they haven't happened yet, they may! If not these, maybe others!

However, anxiety can be a catalyst that leads us to depend on Christ rather than self. He is patiently waiting to take on our burdens, lift our load and give us peace. Peter said "Cast all your anxiety on Him. For He cares for you" (I Peter 5:7). When we leave our island of self reliance and seek Him, we discover that God is willing to replace our anxiety with His supernatural peace. His peace does not eliminate storms but it does provide an adequate shelter.

"You will keep in perfect peace all who trust in you, whose thoughts are fixed on you" (Isaiah 26:3)!

RECORD READ

REFLECT

RESPOND

READ

RECORD

REFLECT

RESPOND

READ

RECORD

REFLECT

RESPOND

FROM ANXIETY TO PEACE
ISAIAH 40:21-31

Day 3

READ

RECORD

REFLECT

RESPOND

PLANNED MEDITATION

Write it out *(Copy it from your Bible)*

Define key words *(Use a dictionary. Page 33)*

Say it again *(Put it in your own words. Page 34)*

CHECK THE MAP

SUMMARIZE KEY IDEAS

Day 6

N

LIFE APPLICATION

1. Express
2. Reflect
3. Assess
4. Claim
5. Apply
(see page 23)

84

CONNECTION

"Because we care, what do we need to know?"

EXPLORATION

"Because God's Word is true, what are you discovering?"

APPLICATION

"Because God's Word is relevant, what is He telling you to do?"

INTERCESSION

"Because God cares, how can we support you in prayer?"

Our quest for peace begins with a right relationship with God. He is the source of real peace. Scripture teaches that before we can have peace from God, we must first have peace with God. Paul said in Romans 5:1, "Since we have been justified through faith, we have peace with God through our Lord Jesus Christ." Christ has brought peace with God through his work for us at the cross.

When we put our faith in Christ, He also gives us the resource of the Holy Spirit to live in us. His Spirit is our divine source of peace. (Galatians 5:22-23) Jesus said when describing the work of His Spirit in John 14:27 (NLT), "I am leaving you with a gift—peace of mind and heart. And the peace I give isn't like the peace the world gives. So don't be troubled or afraid." With the Spirit of peace present within us, we can face our anxieties with a resource that is greater than our circumstances.

However, experiencing the peace of God is not automatic. It requires a response from us. Paul said in Philippians 4:6-7 (NLT), "Don't worry about anything; instead, pray about everything. Tell God what you need, and thank him for all he has done. If you do this, you will experience God's peace, which is far more wonderful than the human mind can understand. His peace will guard your hearts and minds as you live in Christ Jesus. "

Peace becomes a choice. It involves choosing to pray rather than worry; depending on Him rather than self, and giving thanks rather than complaining. God's peace is supernatural. It defies our explanation. It baffles our imagination. But it comes through intentional decisions.

When the peace of God settles our hearts in spite of the circumstances, it sends a message to others. We become ambassadors of peace to a world in conflict. Peace is not found in world systems or even in the freedom from oppression, it is found in a relationship with the Prince of Peace.

READ RECORD

REFLECT

RESPOND

FROM ANXIETY TO PEACE
JOHN 14:23-31

Day 1

87

READ

RECORD

REFLECT

RESPOND

READ
RECORD
REFLECT
RESPOND

FROM ANXIETY TO PEACE
MARK 4:1-20
Day 3

READ

RECORD

REFLECT

RESPOND

PLANNED MEDITATION

Write it out *(Copy it from your Bible)*

Break it down *(See, Search & So What? Page 34)*

Find the bottom line *(The main principle. Page 35)*

CHECK THE MAP

SUMMARIZE KEY IDEAS

Day 6

N ↑

LIFE APPLICATION

1. Express
2. Reflect
3. Assess
4. Claim
5. Apply
(see page 23)

"Because we care, what do we need to know?"

EXPLORATION

"Because God's Word is true, what are you discovering?"

APPLICATION

"Because God's Word is relevant, what is He telling you to do?"

INTERCESSION

"Because God cares, how can we support you in prayer?"

Every person struggles with pride in some way, the kind of pride that comes from our own self elevation, arrogance, conceit, or self-importance. The root of pride lies deep within but can reveal itself in a variety of ways; some are obvious while others are more subtle. It is much easier to see in others than in ourselves. In our culture, pride is often elevated as a virtue and promoted as an asset.

Yet pride or arrogance is found at the top of God's hate list (Proverbs 6:16-19). Pride, we are told, puts us in conflict with God. "For God is opposed to the proud" (I Peter 5:5). Since pride fills us with self-importance, it forces God aside or entirely out.

Pride in a man's world forces "one-up-manship." It fuels competition and promotes self at all costs. Pride is expressed by the attitudes "I can do more and do it better" or "I know more" or "I've already done that" or "I have that figured out". Pride is multi-faceted, but with a singular-self focus.

The Old Testament records the struggles of real people with pride and the consequences of failing to properly deal with it. King Saul is one example where pride affected not only his future but the welfare of his entire family.

Jesus often warned against pride. The early apostles touched on this same issue. In most of the New Testament letters, pride was among the top issues with which new believers needed to deal.

Maturity in Christ results in a change from pride to humility. It is a change not only in behavior but in attitude. Replacing pride with humility is fundamentally a change in how we think about ourselves.

As you reflect on the Bible passages this week, look for the results of pride along with simple but effective solutions to deal with it.

READ

RECORD

REFLECT

RESPOND

FROM PRIDE TO HUMILITY
PHILIPPIANS 2:1-11

Day 1

READ

RECORD

REFLECT

RESPOND

FROM PRIDE TO HUMILITY
1 PETER 5:1-11

Day 3

RECORD READ

REFLECT

RESPOND

Write it out *(Copy it from your Bible)*

Define key words *(Use a dictionary. Page 33)*

Say it again *(Put it in your own words. Page 34)*

LIFE APPLICATION

1. Express
2. Reflect
3. Assess
4. Claim
5. Apply
(see page 23)

CONNECTION

"Because we care, what do we need to know?"

FORUM DISCUSSION

Day 7

EXPLORATION

"Because God's Word is true, what are you discovering?"

APPLICATION

"Because God's Word is relevant, what is He telling you to do?"

INTERCESSION

"Because God cares, how can we support you in prayer?"

In a man's world, where pride is often considered a virtue, humility is often perceived as a weakness. In a highly competitive world, humility is thought of as incompetence, vulnerability, lack of confidence and a liability. It is certainly not a popular quality for men on the fast track of achievement.

Yet Scripture teaches that humility is a supreme value of God's Kingdom. It is presented as a virtue that both pleases God and protects man. It is a character quality that actually builds confidence and establishes respect. Over time, it earns the trust of men and the favor of God.

Humility is a state of mind in response to our true place of dependency upon God and respect for others. We are told that God values it so much that He gives His special favor to those who have it.

"God sets himself against the proud, but he shows favor to the humble" (1 Peter 5:5, NLT).

Pride has been the root of evil from the Garden of Eden to our present day. But just as pride entered our world through Adam, humility came through Jesus. He demonstrated that humility was not weakness but power. He showed that humility was not a liability but a source of redemption. He revealed that humility was part of the very nature of God.

Humility is not optional but rather is essential to the follower of Christ in every culture and in every era. It is a core trait of those who would call themselves His people.

As you meet with God this week, let the following passages guide your understanding of the value and benefit of humility. Grasp how humility was modeled by Jesus as he lived in an arrogant and hostile world. See how humility impacts interpersonal relationships to produce harmony, unity, and community.

READ

RECORD

REFLECT

RESPOND

FROM PRIDE TO HUMILITY
JAMES 4:1-12

Day 1

READ

RECORD

REFLECT

RESPOND

READ

RECORD

REFLECT

RESPOND

FROM PRIDE TO HUMILITY
JOHN 13:1-17

Day 3

READ

RECORD

REFLECT

RESPOND

PLANNED MEDITATION

Write it out *(Copy it from your Bible)*

Break it down *(See, Search & So What? Page 34)*

Find the bottom line *(The main principle. Page 35)*

LIFE APPLICATION

1. Express
2. Reflect
3. Assess
4. Claim
5. Apply
(see page 23)

CONNECTION

"Because we care, what do we need to know?"

EXPLORATION

"Because God's Word is true, what are you discovering?"

APPLICATION

"Because God's Word is relevant, what is He telling you to do?"

INTERCESSION

"Because God cares, how can we support you in prayer?"

An "elephant in the room" refers to a subject that no one wants to discuss yet it is on everyone's mind. There is no bigger "elephant in the room" among men than the topic of purity of life. Every man is wrestling with it but most are hesitant to bring it out into the open. Why is it so hard to discuss? Maybe it's considered too personal and private. Maybe there is the fear of exposure and rejection. Maybe there's a reluctance to face real change.

Jesus, however, was not afraid of this "elephant in the room". In fact, he knew it was so critical, that he would often bring it up--even in public! In the Sermon on the Mount, He raised the purity bar for men when He said, "You have heard that is was said, 'Do not commit adultery.' But I tell you that anyone who looks at a woman lustfully has already committed adultery with her in his heart" (Matthew 5:28).

Peter put it this way: "Be holy yourselves also in all your behavior: because it is written, 'You shall be holy because I am holy'" (1 Peter 1:15, 16). God calls us to comprehensive purity of life because it reflects His nature within us.

Purity of life includes not only actions but also thoughts. It touches the public as well as the private aspects of our lives. It is often hidden immorality that leads to the bigger public failures. Biblical history reveals that the wisest man, the strongest man, and the man after God's own heart failed in moral purity. They, and those around them, suffered the consequences. Satan is no respecter of persons. None of us are immune to his subtle, persistent, and crafty schemes, which are designed to devour and render us useless to the kingdom of God (1 Peter 5:8).

As you begin to reflect this week on God's call to purity of life, let the Scripture, rather than culture, set the standard for purity. Let God reveal more of His moral blueprint for life, even if it makes you uncomfortable.

FROM SEXUAL IMMORALITY TO PURITY
1 THESSALONIANS 4:1-8

RECORD

REFLECT

RESPOND

RECORD

REFLECT

RESPOND

Write it out *(Copy it from your Bible)*

Define key words *(Use a dictionary. Page 33)*

Say it again *(Put it in your own words. Page 34)*

LIFE APPLICATION

1. Express
2. Reflect
3. Assess
4. Claim
5. Apply
(see page 23)

CONNECTION

"Because we care, what do we need to know?"

EXPLORATION

"Because God's Word is true, what are you discovering?"

APPLICATION

"Because God's Word is relevant, what is He telling you to do?"

INTERCESSION

"Because God cares, how can we support you in prayer?"

We are constantly being bombarded with sexually sugges-tive stimuli. We don't have to look for it, it finds us. It perme-ates every form of communication. Somebody's got our number!

What we expose our eyes to determines what "show" is playing in the "theater" of our mind. And the way we think will eventually determine the way we act. Since God has designed men with the sexual drive triggered primarily by the eyes, we are both vulnerable and responsible.

We must learn to aggressively take control of our thought life and those things that affect it. A pure and holy thought life requires establishing Biblically based guidelines for what we allow ourselves to hear and see. It also demands depen-dence on His Spirit to discern truth from the vast amount of trash and garbage that is already floating around in our minds.

Ephesians 4:22-24 says that we must put off the old self, change the way we think, and then put on the new self. This process is best carried out in the context of meeting regu-larly with one or two trusted men who provide perspective, encouragement, and accountability. The result will be signifi-cant transformation toward a pure and holy life.

Is obedience possible in this area? Yes, absolutely! Is it easy? Not usually. What is at stake? Everything! Purity affects our relationship with Christ, our impact for God's kingdom, our marriage, our family, and ultimately our destiny.

Purity is a choice we make. It is a value we must choose. Learning what is at stake, identifying the resources that God provides, and developing the skill to use them is part of our high quest.

Let this week's Scripture passages equip your mind as you put off the old ways and put on what is new.

RECORD

REFLECT

RESPOND

READ
RECORD
REFLECT
RESPOND

FROM SEXUAL IMMORALITY TO PURITY
1 PETER 1:13-21

Day 2

READ

RECORD

REFLECT

RESPOND

RECORD

REFLECT

RESPOND

Write it out (Copy it from your Bible)

Break it down (See, Search & So What? Page 34)

Find the bottom line (The main principle. Page 35)

PLANNED MEDITATION

N
↑
_____
_____
_____
_____
_____
_____
_____
_____
_____
_____
_____
_____
_____
_____
_____
_____
_____
_____
_____
_____
_____
_____
_____
_____

LIFE APPLICATION

1. Express
2. Reflect
3. Assess
4. Claim
5. Apply
(see page 23)

_____
_____
_____
_____
_____
_____

CONNECTION

"Because we care, what do we need to know?"

EXPLORATION

"Because God's Word is true, what are you discovering?"

APPLICATION

"Because God's Word is relevant, what is He telling you to do?"

INTERCESSION

"Because God cares, how can we support you in prayer?"

His Image

HIGHQUEST II
APPENDIX

The Appointment With God life skill is a spiritual habit or discipline that will equip you for a lifetime of walking with Christ. Once you learn how to use it, you can adapt it to fit your quest for knowing Christ no matter where you are along your spiritual journey.

Meeting regularly with Christ is like using a compass. A compass has been standard equipment for travelers for centuries. A compass is especially critical for anyone climbing in the mountains because it gives a reliable point of reference. It allows a climber to keep on track no matter what the conditions are around him. Likewise, your AWG will allow you to check your spiritual position, get your bearings and chart your course as you keep your eyes and heart on Christ.

An AWG is a regular, daily time when you relate with Christ through his Word and prayer. This spiritual discipline has been called by many names, but it has consistently proven essential throughout Christian history in every age and culture.

We are accustomed to making appointments for just about everything. Appointments insure that intentions get carried out. Making an appointment helps us commit to a particular course of action. We often intend to get time alone with God but fail to pull it off. We think it's a good idea and even have it on our "do list". But until we get it on our appointment calendar, it remains just a good intention.

Establishing the habit of meeting with God on a regular basis is foundational to developing a deeper relationship with Christ. Friendships develop with dialogue and shared experiences over time. Meeting in corporate worship is no substitute for individual interaction with God. Periodic time with God is not as effective as consistent time with him.

Imagine your frustration if a friend says he wants to meet with you but never shows up. The Bible presents God as intensely eager to meet with us. He waits, hopes, even calls to see if we are coming. It's time we kept the appointment. The prophet Isaiah said, "Seek the Lord while you can find him. Call on him now while he is near."

HighQuest I will teach you the basic elements of this important life skill. But it will take practice, discipline, and perseverance to make it a habit in your life.

Learning a new skill or habit is awkward initially. It usually takes a number of tries and a few falls to learn to ride a bike. At first we don't even care where we are going. Our goal is to stay vertical! But once we master the skill, we no longer think about balance or steering. We are free to keep our heads up, experience what's around us, and enjoy the journey. In the same way, mastering new spiritual skills gives us greater freedom and joy as we develop our relationship with God.

Initially you may find that 10 to 15 minutes a day is adequate for your AWG. But as you develop your relationship with Christ, your desire to spend time in his presence will increase. On the other hand, some days you will find it tough to get even 10 to 15 minutes. Don't make the mistake of measuring your relationship with Christ based on the performance of the discipline. Disciplines are necessary, but they are not a merit system with God.

Keep your eyes and heart on Christ and let the disciplines and skills become like the sails on a ship. In the same way the sails catch the wind and power the ship, so also the spiritual disciplines catch the wind of the Spirit of God. He is the power behind our quest to follow Christ.

Strategy

In order to establish a consistent AWG, you need to establish a realistic time, place and plan.

• Time

Identify a consistent time during the day when you can get alone with God. It is best to build the AWG habit around the same time each day. There is no time that is right or wrong but there is a time that will work best for you. It needs to be a time when you are alert, which may be the first thing in the day for some or at the end of the day for others. The best time for you may be over lunch or before work. Discover what works best for you and stick with it.

The length of time spent each day in an AWG is not as critical as the habit of doing it consistently. Begin with 15 minutes until it becomes a habit. Once you have developed the habit, it is easy to expand it as needed.

• Place

You need to identify a place where you can meet with God privately, regularly and free from distractions. It may be a special room or a favorite chair in your home or office. You will need to be flexible because the best place will often change as circumstances change.

• Plan

It is important to develop a simple plan that will allow an effective dialogue with Christ and promote consistency. You can enhance and modify your plan as you gain confidence. HighQuest I introduces you to a plan that has been used throughout Christian history by men and women of all ages and every culture. It is simple and can be easily adapted to changing lifestyles.

Step 1: Read

Begin your AWG by reading a passage of Scripture. It can be a few verses or a whole chapter. Usually it is best to limit the reading to a few verses in order to have time to reflect over them. The purpose of an AWG is to meet with God not to gain a lot of information. We suggest using an inexpensive Bible for your AWG. As you read over the passage several times, mark words and ideas that stand out to you.

Each week in HighQuest I, you will read five passages with a common theme. The goal is to be consistent in your AWG for at least 5 out of 7 days. Once you finish HighQuest, you can continue with your AWG using your own reading selections.

Remember the passages given are not to limit you but to start you. You may read more than suggested or not as much. The AWG is designed for you to stop and dialogue with God as he speaks through his Word. It is not designed to be a comprehensive Bible study. Rather it is designed to help you connect with Christ on a regular and personal basis – to sit as his feet and listen to his words.

Step 2: Record
Once you have read the passage over a few times, note the verse or phrase that God seems to emphasize. It may be a complete verse, a statement or a phrase. Write this out, word for word, in your AWG journal page. Recording this Biblical statement will help you focus your thoughts and listen to God. Selecting one verse or phrase helps to corral a wandering mind and sharpen your focus.

Step 3: Reflect
Stop and think about what God is saying to you from what you have recorded. Ask questions to gain insight and understanding into God's truth. For example ask "what, why, how or when" type questions. You are looking not only for what the passage says but what it means. You first record the facts (what does it say?) and then reflect to understand the implications (what does it say to me?). Remember you are putting your heart in a position to listen to God. Don't be afraid to be

silent and tune in to the quiet voice of the Holy Spirit.

As you reflect, write down your ideas and thoughts on the journal page. Often God will give you something specific that you need to apply to your life. When He does, write it down as well.

Journaling has many advantages. It helps you clarify and formulate concisely what you are hearing from God in Scripture. Thoughts take on shape and stick in your mind as you write them down. Keeping this kind of a journal becomes a way to log your journey with God. Journaling allows you to remember patterns and major lessons God is working out in your life.

Step 4: Respond

Once you have reflected on God's Word, it is important to pray over what you have just read and thought about. Write out a short 1-2 sentence prayer that expresses back to God what you have heard him say. Allow what you've read to guide your prayer time. You will also want to pray over issues and people who will be part of your day's agenda.

What People are Saying About HighQuest

Businessmen

I am living a more authentic Christian life in my home and in my business because of the effect of the HighQuest series.

  Chris Miller, President LANIT Consulting, Inc., Oregon

"HighQuest" has been a blessing to our men's ministry. It has just the right balance for digging into the Scripture with a format to build strong godly relationships. The result has been a deeper relationship with God and with each other.

  Bryan Gilbert, President, Alpha-Omega Industries, Missouri

Pastors

For years I struggled to get my church board members to develop a consistent devotional life with little success. The "HighQuest" materials were the first tools that brought all the elements together that helped them to develop a consistent and deeper walk with Christ. The easy to follow format, the accountability meetings, and the heart and skill development helped to connect us not only to God but to each other. We now look forward to meeting with each other to share what God is teaching us. I recommend this tool to anyone who wants a simple but powerful tool for equipping people to connect with God and each other.

  John Grussi, Pastor Peninsula Christian Fellowship, California

"HighQuest" has brought simple spiritual disciplines into the hands of our men in practical ways. I see men wrestling with God, their world, and themselves in life changing ways. God is more real and closer than they had ever thought...and the Scriptures are coming alive to them in fresh ways. As a pastor I love seeing God's people grow spiritually. I am convinced that if men can grow and mature spiritually it will have a Christ-honoring impact in the home, the neighborhoods at church, and around the world.

  Matt Uldrich , Director of Men's Ministry, Catalina Foothills Church, Arizona

Navigator Staff

I had been searching for an effective tool to help men develop a consistent appointment with God when I came across the "HighQuest" series. There are lots of activities for men that are all very helpful but generally, do not get men into the Word on a daily, consistent and personal basis. Using "HighQuest", I am now watching men's lives being transformed week by week as we share together what God has spoken to us about during the week.

  Roger Fleming, Navigator Staff, Colorado

I have found that "HighQuest" covers the spiritual needs for discipleship training wherever a person may be in his journey. From those that are just coming to a relationship with Christ, to those who have reached a plateau in their growth, or for those who have a hunger to grow even deeper....no matter what the need, there seems to be a "HighQuest" book that is ideal for the situation. I have witnessed it changing other men's lives and have experienced it in my own. It seems to be the ideal tool for establishing a church discipleship training program.

  Bill Penkethman, Navigator Staff, Missouri

About the Authors

HighQuest: Men on a Mission was developed by a team of Navigator staff who share a common vision for reaching and equipping men for Christ and His kingdom. Together they represent over 160 years of discipling experience.

Ron Bennett

Graduating from Iowa State University with a degree in Aerospace Engineering, Ron served as an officer in the US Army including a tour in Viet Nam. He has served as a Navigator staff in campus, military, and community ministries. Ron is the author of *Intentional Disciplemaking* (NavPress 2001). He coauthored *Opening the Door* and *The Adventure of Discipling Others* (NavPress 2003). Ron and his wife, Mary, wrote *Beginning the Walk* (NavPress 2005). Ron and Mary live in Kansas City where he serves as regional director for The Navigators Church Discipleship Ministry.

Larry Glabe

Larry graduated from Illinois State University with a degree in Secondary Education. He taught high school in Chicago before coming on staff with The Navigators. Larry served as The Navigator campus director at the University of Northern Iowa and the University of Missouri. He directed the Navigators Business and Professional Men's Ministry in central Missouri and served as chaplain for the Missouri Tigers. He coauthored *Opening the Door* (NavPress). Larry and his wife, Kathy, live in Columbia, MO where he serves as a spiritual coach to business men and directs The Navigator Church Discipleship Ministry in central Missouri.

Chuck Strittmatter

Chuck was raised in southwest Iowa. He served in the U.S. Navy before getting his BS degree at the University of Northern Iowa. He joined The Navigators staff and has served as campus director at Kansas State University, regional director in New England, country director of Australia, and field director for Iowa/Nebraska as well as coaching CoMission teams in Russia and Ukraine. God took Chuck home in November, 2009 after fighting cancer. He finished his course of faith well and is deeply missed. Chuck is survived by his wife, Nancy.

Bob Walz

Bob grew up in Nebraska and graduated from the University of Nebraska with a major in Zoology/Pre-Medicine. He served with The Navigators at Hosei University in Tokyo, Japan as well as led collegiate ministries at the University of Iowa, Kansas State University, and the University of Nebraska. He developed *The Field Survival Kit* which is a CD of materials for helping people minister to others. Distributed widely to service personnel in Iraq, many of the items are available at: www.navresources.com . Bob also coauthored a devotional for high school athletes called *Get in the Game*. Bob and his wife, Sandy, live in Lincoln, NE where he serves with The Navigators National Collegiate Ministry.

The HighQuest Series: Men on a Mission
www.highquest.info

Track I Know Christ Deeply	Track II Reflect Christ Authentically	Track III Share Christ Intentionally
a. His Works Understanding who God is and how it impacts our new identity in Christ.	**a. His Image** Reflecting the reality of Christ through a look at transformation and 4 major character traits.	**a. His Heart** Looking at God's heart for lost and broken people. Learn the skills sets for sharing the gospel.
b. His Ways Looking at the paths God wants us to take along our spiritual journey.	**b. His Calling** Exploring Christ's call to discipleship, looking at the 5 marks of a disciple.	**b. His Commission** Learning to expand His kingdom by discipling others.
c. His Glory Understanding the attributes of God.	**c. His Nature** Reflecting Christ-like qualities built on the foundation of faith.	**c. His Story** Learning to be a spiritual guide (Sherpa) to help men understand the gospel.

Spanish version of His Works

The *HighQuest Journal* allows you to select your own passages for the AWG yet continue in the HighQuest I format.

Transformation

Do not conform any longer to the pattern of this world, but be transformed by the renewing of your mind. Then you will be able to test and approve what God's will is--his good, pleasing and perfect will.

Romans 12:2 NIV

Peace

Do not be anxious about anything, but in everything, by prayer and petition, with thanksgiving, present your requests to God.

Philippians 4:6 NIV

Name _____

Phone _____

Humility

Do nothing out of selfish ambition or vain conceit, but in humility consider others better than yourselves.

Philip. 2:3 NIV

Purity

It is God's will that you should be sanctified: that you should avoid sexual immorality;

1 Thessalonians 4:3 NIV

Patience

My dear brothers, take note of this: Everyone should be quick to listen, slow to speak and slow to become angry,

James 1:19 NIV